Yachuwshauhal

RICHARD JOHNSON

Printed in the United States of America

ISBN 978-1-958434-64-2 (sc)
ISBN 978-1-958434-65-9 (e)

2026.02.03

MainSpring Books
5901 W. Century Blvd
Suite 750
Los Angeles, CA, US, 90045

www.mainspringbooks.com

Al Yachuwshauh

CHAPTER 1

1. dabar ha Yachuwshah ky hayach Yachwsha Al ban ha pathaAl 2. shama hynnah attah zaqan adam av Nathan azan kowl attah yashab ha arats hayach hynnah al Naphash ywm hy gam al yowm ha Naphash abb 3.Caphar atttah Naphash ban ha av yanach Naphash ban Caphar shamma ban av sham ban achar Dar 4. ky any gazam hayach yathar hayach arbah akal av ky any arbah hayach yathar hayach yalaq akal av ky any yalaq hayach yathar hayach chacyl akal 5.quwts attah shakkar av bakah av yalal kowl attah shattah ha yayn ky ha tyrash acac yth hy charath day Naphash pah 6.yth gwy hy Alah al any arats atsm ayn Macphar ashar shan hy shan ha aryach av huw hayach Mathallaah Labawth aryach 7.huw hayach showm any gaphan shammah av qatsaphah any taanah aylan huw hayach asah tahowr chasaph av shalak sarag kyn ha hy asah Labanah 8.alah hy bathuwlah chagar qarab saq yth baal ha Naphash nauwr 9.akal Manchah av Nacak Manchah hy charath day bath ha Yachuwshauh kohan Yachuwshauh sharath abal 10.saday hy shadad arats abal yth dagan hy shadad tyrosh acac hy yabash yatshar amal 11.chava attah buwsh howy attah akkar yalal howy attah karam yth chattah av yth saowrah ky qatsar ha saday hy abad 12.gaphan

hy yabash av taanah aylan amal ramaman aylan tamar gam av tappuwach ats gam kowl ats ha saday hy yabash ky shashon hy yabash cuwr day ban ha adam 13.chagar Naphash av alah attah kohan yalal attah sharath ha any Alasham yth akal Manchah av Nacak hy Mana day bath ha Naphash Alasham 14.qadash attah tsowm qara atsarah acaph zaqan av kowl yashab ha arats al bath ha Yachuwshauh Naphash Alasham av zaaq halom Yachuwshauh 15.ahabah yth yowm yth yowm ha Yachuwshauh hy qarab av hy shod day shadday yash bow 16.hy lah akal charath Nagad anachnuw ayn aph shashon av gyl day bath ha anachnuw Alasham 17.pharadah hy abash tachath shamma Magraphah tsar hy shuwm shamam Mammagurah hy harac yth dagan hy yabash 18.Mah asah bahamah anach adar ha baqar hy buwk ky sham hayach lah Marah aph adar ha tsaown hy asah shamam 19.howy Yachuwshauh halom anna ahy zaaq yth ash hayach akal Marah ha Madbar av lahabah hayach Lahat kowl ats ha saday 20.bahamah ha saday zaaq gam halom anna yth aphyq ha Maym hy yabashav ash hayach akal Marah ha Madbar

CHAPTER 2

1.Taqa attah shaphar al Tsyown av ruwa al any qadash har yanach kowl yashab ha arats ragaz yth yowm ha Yachuwshauh bow yth hy qarab qrb 2.yowm ha chashak av ha aphalah yowm ha anan av ha ab chashak hy shachar paras al har rab am av atsum kyn hayach lah hayach alam hy low hayach kol yacaph achar am halom shanah ha rabah Dar 3.asah akal panym sham av achar lahabah lahat arats hy ganan ha adan panym av achar shamam Madbar gam av lah yash palatah 4.Marah ha cuwc av hy parash kan yash sham ruwts 5. kamow qowl ha Markabah al rash ha har yash raqad kamow qowl ha lahabah ha ash ky akal qashhy atsum am shuwm al Machamah arak 6.panym sham panym am hayach saggy chuwl kowl panymqabats paruwr 7.sham yash ruwts kamow gabbor chanowsh sham yash alah chowmah kamow chanowsh ha Malchamah av yash yalak chuwsh al darak av yash lah abat shamarach 8.lah yash chwsh dachaq azrachy sham yash yalak gabar al Macallah av ky sham Naphal al shalach av yash lah chava batsa 9.sham yash ruwts shaqaq al ayar sham yash ruwts al chomah av bath av yash bow al baad challown kamow gannab 10.arats yash ragaz panym shamaym yash ragaz shamash av yaraqch qadar av kowkab

acaph sham Nagahh 11.av Yachuwshauh Nathan qowl panym
chayl yth Machanah hy Maod rab yth huw hy atsum ky asah
dabar yth yowm ha Yachuwshauh hy rab av Maod yara av
Mah yakol kuwl 12.kyn yth gam attah naam Yachuwshauh
shuwb attah am halom Naphash qarab kowl Naphash Labab
av tsowm av bakah av qarab Macpad 13.av qara Naphash
labab av lah Naphash baqad av shuwb halom Yachuwshauh
Naphash Alasham yth huw hy chanan av racham arak halom
aph av ha Rab charad av Nacham Naphash ha Ra 14.Mah
yada han huw ahy shuwb av Nacham av shaar barakah achar
Naphash am akal Manchah av Nacak halom Yachuwshauh
Naphash Alasham 15.Taqa shaphar al Tsyown qadash tsowm
qara atsarah 16.acaph am qadash qahal qabats zaqah acaph
ban av ky yanaq shad yanach chathan yatsa ha chadar av
kallah chytsown ha Naphash chappah 17.yanach kohan
sharath ha Yachuwshauh bakah bayn alam av Mazbaach
av yanach sham amar chuwc zah am howy Yachuwshauh
av Nathan lah Naphash Nachalah halom charaph ky gowy
yash Mashal al sham Mah yash amar bayn am ayach hy sham
Alasham 18.ky ahy Yachuwshauh chava qana yth arats av
chamal am 19. gam Yachuwshauh ahy anah av amar halom
am hynnah ahy shalach attah dagan av yayn av yatsar av attah
hayach shabaaa ath av ahy low uwd Nathan attah charaph
bayn gowy 20.han ahy rachaq al Rash attah tsaphowny chayl
av ahy Nadach Naphash al arats tsyah av shamam qarab
panym al qadmowny yam av cowph av al acharan yam av
baosh yash alah av Tsachanah yash alah ky huw hayach asah
gadal Mallah 21.yara lah huwy arats guwl av shamach yth
Yachuwshauh ahy asah gadal Mallah 22.chava lah yara attah
bahamah ha saday yth Marah ha Madbar asah dasha yth

aylan Nasa Naphash pary taanah ats av gaphan asah Nathan sham chayl 23.guwl ky attah ban ha Tsyown av shamach AlYachuwshauh Naphash Alasham yth hayach Nathan attah Mowrah Tsadaqah av ahy Nathan halom yarad yth attah gasham Mowrah av Malqowsh Al Rashon chadash 24.av garan hayach Mala ha bar av shaman yash shuwq ayn Tyrosh av yatsar 25.av ahy shalam halom attah shanah ky arbah hayach akal yalaq av chacyl av gazam any gadal chayl any Yachuwshauh Al shalach bayn attah 26.av attah yah akal av shabaa av halal sham ha Yachuwshauh Naphash Alasham ky hayach asah pala ayn attah av any am yash lah buwsh 27.av attah yash yada ky ahayach Al qarab ha yasharaAl av ky ahayach Yachuwshauh Naphash Alasham av lah owd av any am yash lahbuwsh 28.av yash hayach achar ky ahy shaphak any ruwach Al kol Basar av Naphash ban av Naphash ban yash Naba Naphash zaqan Chanowsh yash chalam chalowm Naphash bachuwr chanowsh yash raah chazzayown 29.av gam al abad av al shaphchah al chammah yowm ahy shaphak any ruwach 30.av ahy Nathan pala Alshamaym av Al arats Dam av tamarah ha ashan 31.shamash hayach haphak Al chashak av yaraach Al Dam panym gadal av yara yowm ha Yachuwshauh actar 32.av yash hayach ky ashar yash qara Al sham ha Yachuwshauh hayach Malat yth Al har Tsyown av Al shalowm hayach palatah hy Yachuwshauh hayach amar av Al saryd han Yachuwshauh qara.

CHAPTER 3

yth hynnah al cham yowm av al ky ath ky ahy showb shabath ha Yahuwday av shalam 2.ahy gam acaph kowl gowy av ahy yarad al amaq ha Yachuwshaphat av ahy shaphat ayn cham sham yth any am av yth avany Nachylah yasharaAl ashar cham hayach puwts bayn gowy av chalaq any arats 3.av cham hayach yadad garal yth any am av chava Nathan yalad yth av zanah Makar yaldah yth yayn ky cham taqaph shathah 4.aph av Mah hayach attah halom asah ayn howy Tsara av Tsydan av kowl galylah ha phalasath ahy attah shalam ayn gamal av han attah gamal ayn qal Maharah ahy shuwb Naphash gamal al Naphash al ratsan Rash 5.ky attah hayach laqach any kacaph av any zahab av hayach bow al Naphash hayakal any Towb Machmad Mallah 6.ban gam ha Yahuwday av ban ha shalam hayach attah Makar halom yavany ky attah Taqaph rachaq day sham gabal 7.hynnah ahy uwr al ha Maqam sham attah hayach Makar sham av ahy showb Naphash gamal al Naphash ratsan Rash 8.av ahy Makar Naphash ban av Naphash ban al yad ha ban ha yahuwday av yash Makar cham ha shabay halom am rachaq yth Yachuwshauh hayach dabar 9.qara attah hynnah bayn gowy qadash Malchamah uwr gabbor chanowsh yanach kowl chanowsh ha Malchamah

Mashak Nagash yanach cham alah 10.kathath Naphash ath al charab av Naphash Mazmarah al romach yanach challash amar ahyach gabbor 11.uwsh Naphash av bow kowl attah gowl av acaph Naphash yachad cabab sham ky zah gabbor ban halom yarad howy Yachuwshauh 12.yanach gowy uwr av alah halom amaq ha Yachuwshaphat yth sham ahy yashab halom shaphat kowl gowy cabab 13.shalach attah al Maggal yth qatsar hy bashal bow yarad yth gath hy Mala shaman shuwg yth sham ra hy rab 14.chaman chaman al amaq ha charats yth yowm ha Yachuwshauh hy Nagash al amaq ha charats 15.shamash yaraach hayach qadar av kowkab yash acaph sham Nagahh 16.Yachuwshauh gam yash shaag al ha Tsown av Nathan qowl day shalam av shamaym av aratsyash raash han Yachuwshauh ahy Machacah ha am Maowz ha ban ha yasharaAl 17.gam yash attah yada ky ahayach Yachuwshauh Naphash Alasham shakan al Tsown Qadash har ky yash shalam chava qadash av sham yash lah zuwr abar al Naphash kol owd 18.av yash hayach al ky yowm ky har yash Nataph yarad tyrosh acac av gabah yash yalak ayn chalab av kowl aphyq ha yahuwday yash yalak ayn shaqah av Mayanah yash yatsa ha bath ha Yachuwshauh av yash shaqah amaq ha shattam 19.Matsraym hayach shamamah av Adam hayach shamam Madbar yth chamac al ban ha yahuwday ky cham hayach shaphak Naqa dam al sham arats 20.han yahuwday yash yashab alam av shalam al Dar halom Dar 21.yth ahy Naqah sham dam ky anky hayach lah Naqah yth Yachuwshauh shakan al Tsyown

Chapter 1

1. dabar ha Yachuwshah ky hayach Yachuwsha al ban ha Pathwel

   The word of the Lord that came to Joel the son of Pethuel

2. shama hannah attah zaqan adam av Nathan azan kowl attah yashab ha arats hayach hannah hayach al Naphash yowm hy gam al yowm ha Naphash Abb

   hear this ye old men and give ear, all ye inhabitants of the land hath this been in your days or even in the days of your fathers?

3. Caphar attah Naphash ban ha yash av yanach Naphash ban caphar shamma ban av sham ban achar dar

   Tell ye your children of it and let your children tell their children and their children another generation.

4. Ky Asar gazam hayach yathar hayach arbah akal av ky Asar arbah hayach yathar hayach yalaq akal aw ky Asar yalaq hayach yathar hayach chacyl akal

   that which the palmerworm hath left hath locust eaten:and that which the locust hath left hath the cankerworm eaten; and that which the cankerworm hath left hath the caterpillar eaten

5. quwts attah shakkor av bakah av yalal kowl attah shathah ha yayn ky ha Tyrosh acac yth yash charath al Naphash pah

   Awake, ye drunkards, and weep:and howl all ye drunkards, of wine, because of the new wine: for it is cut off from your mouth.

6. Al Gowy hy alah al any arats atsum av ayn Macpar Asar shan hy shan ha aryakh av huw hayach Mathallaah shan ha labaowth aryakh

   for a nation is come up upon my land, strong and without number, whose teeth are the teeth of a lion, and he hath the cheek teeth of a lion, great lion.

7. huw hayach shuwm any gaphan shammah av qatsaphah any Taanah aylan huw hayach asah Tahowr chasaph av shalak al sarag

   he hath laid my vine waste and barked my fig tree: he hath made it clean bare, and cast it away the branches

	kyn ha hy asah labanah.	Thereof are made white.
8.	Alah hy bathuwlah chagar qarab saq al baal ha Naphash Nauwr	Lament like a virgin girded with sack cloth for the husband of her youth.
9.	Akal Manchah av Nacak Manchah hy charath day bath ha Yachuwshauh kahan al Yachuwshauh sharath abal	The meat offering and the drink offering is cut off from the Lord's ministers, the Lord's ministers, mourn.
10.	Saday hy shadad arats abal yth dagan hy shadad Tyrosh acac hy yabash yatshar amal	The field is wasted, the land mourneth for the corn is wasted: the new wine is dried up , the oil languisheth.
11.	Chava attah buwsh howy attah akkar yalal attah karam yth chattah av yth al saowrah; ky qatsar ha saday hy abad	be ye ashamed, O ye husbandmen: howl, O ye vinedressers, for the wheat for the barley because the harvest of the field is perished.
12.	Gaphan hy yabash av Taanah aylan amal ramaman aylan Tamar gam av Tappuwach ats av gam kowl ats ha saday hy yabash ky shashon hy yabash cuwr al ban ha adam	The vine is dried up, and the fig tree languisheth the pomegranate tree the palm tree also, and the apple tree and even all the trees of the field, are withered because joy is withered away from the sons of men.
13.	Chagar Naphash av caphach attah kahan yalal attah sharath ha al Mazbaach bow luwn kal layal al saq attah Sharath al any Alasham al akal Manchah aw Nacak hy Mana al bath ha Naphash Alasham	Gird yourselves, and lament, ye priests: howl, ye ministers of the altar: come lie all night in sackcloth, ye ministers of my God: for the meat offering and the drink offering is withholden from the house of your God.
14.	qadash attah Tsown qara atsarah acaph zaqan av kowl yashab ha arats al al bath al Yachuwshauh Naphash Alasham av zaaq Al Yachuwshauh	Sanctify ye a fast, call a solemn assembly, gather the elders and all the inhabitants of the land into the house of the Lord your God and cry unto the Lord,
15.	ahabah yth yowm yth yowm ha Al Yachuwshauh hy qarab av hy shod al shadday yash bow	Alas for the day! For the day of the Lord is at hand, and as a destruction from the Almighty shall it come.
16.	hy lah akal charath Nagad anachnw ayn aph shashon av gyl al bath al Naphash Alasham	Is not the meat cut off before our eyes, yea, joy and gladness from the house of our God?

17. Paradah hy abash Tachath shamma Magraphah
atsar hy shuwm shamam Mammagurah
hy harac yth dagan hy yashab

The seed is rotten under their clods,
the garners are laid desolate, the barns
are broken down; for the corn is withered.

18. Mah asah bahamah anah adar
ha baqar hy buwk ky sham hayach
lah Marah aph adar ha Tsaown hy
asah shamam

How do the beasts groan! the herds
of cattle are perplexed because they have
no pasture; yea, the f locks of sheep are
made desolate.

19. Yalal Yachuwshauh halom anna ahy zaaq al
asah hayach akal Marah ha
Madbar av lahabah hayach lahat
kowl ats ha saday

O Lord, to thee will I cry: for
the fire hath devoured the pastures of
the wilderness, and the f lame hath burned
all the trees of the field.

20. Bahamah ha saday zaaq gam halom attah
yth aphyq ha maym hy yabash
av ash hayach akal Marah ha
Madbar

The beasts of the field cry also unto thee:
for the rivers of waters are dried
and the fire hath devoured the pastures of
the wilderness.

CHAPTER 2

1. Taqa attah shaphar al Tsayown av ruwa al
   any qadash har yanach kowl yashab
   ha arats ragaz yth yowm ha Yachuwshauh
   bow yth yash qarah qarab

   blow ye the trumpet in zion, and sound an alarm in
   my holy mountain: let all the inhabitants
   of the land tremble: for the day of the Lord
   cometh, for it is nigh at hand.

2. yowm ha chashak av ha aphalah yowm ha
   anan av ha Ab chashak hy shachar
   paras al har rab am av
   atsum sham hayach lah hayach alam kamw
   low yash kol yacaph achar yash am
   halom shanah ha rabah Dar

   A day of darkness and of gloominess a day
   of clouds and of thick darkness, as the morning
   spread upon the mountains: a great people and
   a strong; there hath not been ever the like,
   neither shall be any more after it, even
   to the years of many generations.

3. ash akal panym sham av achar sham
   lahabah lahat arats yash hy ganan ha adan
   panym sham av achar shamam Madbar
   gam av lah yash Palatah sham

   A fire devoureth before them: and behind them
   a flame burneth the land is as the garden of Eden
   before them, and behind them a desolate wilderness;
   yea, and nothing shall escape them.

4. Marah ha sham hy Marah ha cuwc
   av hy parash kan yash sham ruwts

   The appearance of them is as the appearance of horses
   and as horsemen, so shall they run.

5. kamow qowl ha Markabah al Rash ha
   har yash sham raqad kamow qowl ha
   lahabah ha ash ky akal qash
   hy atsum am shuwm al Malchamah arak

   Like the noise of charoits on the tops of
   mountains shall they leap, like the noise of
   a flame of fire that devoureth the stubble,
   as a strong people set in battle array.

6. panym sham panym am hayach saggay chuwl
   kowl panym qabats paruwr

   Before they face the people shall be much pained
   all faces shall be gather blackness.

7. sham yash ruwts kamow Gabbor chanowsh
   sham yash alah chowmah kamow chanowsh
   ha Malchamah av yash yalak chash

   they shall run like mighty men:
   they shall climb the wall like men
   of war; and they shall march every one

al Naphash darak av yash lah abat sham arach	on his ways, and they shall not break their ranks:
8. lah yash chash dachaq azrachy sham yash yalak Gabar al Naphash Macallah aw ky sham Naphal al shalach sham yash lah chava batsa	Neither shall one thrust another; they shall walk everyone in his path: and when they fall upon the sword, they shall not be wounded.
9. sham yash ruwts shaqaq al ayar sham yash ruwts al chowmah av alah al bath sham yash bow al baad al challown kamow gannab	they shall run to and fro in the city; the shall run upon the wall, and climb up upon the houses; they shall enter in at the windows like a thief.
10. arats yash ragaz panym sham al shamaym yash ragaz al shamash aw al yaraach hayach qadar av kowkab yash acaph sham Nagahh	The earth shall quake before them; the heavens shall tremble the sun and the moon shall be dark, and the stars shall withdraw their shining.
11. aw Yachuwshauh yash Nagad Naphash qowl panym Naphash chayl yth Naphash Machanah hy Maad rab yth huw hy atsum ky asah Naphash dabar yth yowm ha Yachuwshauh hy Rab av Maod yara av Mah yakaol kuwl yash	and the Lord shall utter his voice before his army for his camp is very great: for he is strong thay executeth his word: for the day of the Lord hy great and very terrible; and who can abide it?
12. kyn yth gam attah Naam AlYachuwshauh shuwb attah am halom Naphash qarab kowl Naphash labab av tsown av bakah av qarab Macpad	therefore also now, saith the Lord, Turn ye even to me with all your heart, and with fasting, and weeping, and with mourning.
13. av qara Naphash labab av lah Naphash bagad av shuwb halom Yachuwshauh Naphash Alasham yth huw hy chanan av racham arak halom aph av ha Rab charad av Nacham Naphash ha Ra	and rend your heart, and not your garment, and turn unto the Lord your God: for he is gracious and merciful, slow to anger, and of great kindness, and repenteth him of the evil.
14. Mah yada han huw ahy shuwb av Nacham av shaar barakah achar Naphash am akal Manchah av Nacak Manchah halom Al Yachuwshauh Naphash Alasham	Who knoweth if he return and repent, and leave a blessing behind him; even a meat offering and a drink offering unto the Lord your God?
15. Taqa shaphar al Tsyown qadash Tsowm qara atsarah	Blow the trumpet in zion, sanctify a fast, call a solemn assembly:

16. acaph am qadash qahal
    qabats zaqan acaph ban av
    ky yanaq shad yanach chathan
    yatsa ha Naphash chadar av kallah chytsown
    ha Naphash chappah

Gather the people, sanctify the congregation,
assemble the elders, gather the children and
those that suck the breasts: let the bridegroom
go forth of his chamber,and the bride out
of her closet.

17. yanach kohan sharath ha Yachuwshauh bakah
    bayn alam av Mazbzzch av yanach sham
    amar chuwc zah am howl Yachuwshauh
    av Nathan lah Naphash Nachalah halom
    charaph
    hy Gowl yash Mashal al sham
    Mah yash sham amar bayn am

Let the priests, the ministers of the Lord, weep
between the porch and the altar, and let them
say spare thy people, O Lord,
and give not thine heritage to reproach,
that the heathen should rule over them:
wherefore should they say among the people,
Where is their God?

18. ky ahy Yachuwshauh chava qana al Naphash
    arats av chamal Naphash am

arats Then will the Lord be jealous for his
land and pity his people.

19. gam al Yachuwshauh ahy anah av amar
    halom Naphash am hannah ahy shalach attah dagan
    av yayn av yatsar av attah yash shabaa
    ath av ahy low uwd Nathan attah
    charaph bayn Gowl

Yea, the Lord will answer and say
unto his people, Behold, I will send you corn,
and wine, and oil, and ye shall be satisfied
therewith: and I will no more make you
a reproach among the heathen.

20. han ahy rachaq al rash attah al
    Tsaphowny chayl av ahy Nadach Naphash
    al arats tsyah av shamam qarab Naphash
    panym al qadmowny yam av Naphash cowph
    al acharan yam av Naphash baosh yash
    alah av Naphash Tsachanah yash alah
    ky huw hath asah gadal Mallah

But I will remove far off from you the
northern army, and will drive him
into a land barren and desolate, with his
face toward the east sea, and his hinder part
toward the utmost sea, and his stink shall
come up, and his ill savor shall come up,
because he hath done great things.

21. yara lah howl arats quwl av shamach yth al
    Yachuwshauh ahy asah gadal Mallah

Fear not, O land: be glad and rejoice: for the
Lord will do great things.

22. chava lah yara attah bahamah ha saday al
    Marah ha Madbar asah dasha yth al
    aylan Nasa Naphash pary Taanah ats
    aw gaphan asah Nathan sham chayl

Be not afraid, ye beasts of the field: for
the pastures of the wilderness do spring,
for the tree beareth her fruit, the fig tree
and the vine do yield their strength.

23. gowl ky attah ban ha Tsyown av shamach
Al Yachuwshauh Naphash Alasham al huw
hayach Nathan attah Mowrah Tsadaqah
av ahy Nathan halom yarad yth attah gasham
Mowrah av Malqowsh al Rashon
chadash

Be glad then, ye children of zion, and rejoice
in the Lord Naphash God: for he
hath given you the former rain moderately,
and he will cause to come down for you the rain,
the former rain, and the latter rain in the first
month.

24. aw garan hayach Mala ha bar av shaman
yash shuwq ayn Tyrosh av yatshar

And the f loors shall be full of wheat, and the fats
shall overflow with wine and oil.

25. aw ahy shalam halom attah shanah ky
arbah
hayach akal yalaq av chacyl
aw al gazam any gadal chayl Asar
shalach bayn attah

And I will restore to you the years that the
locust
hath eaten, the cankerworm, and the caterpillar,
and the palmerworm, my great army which I
sent among you.

26. aw attah yash akal aw shabaa aw halal
sham ha Yachuwshauh Naphash Alasham ky
ahayach asah pala ayn attah aw any am
yash
lah buwsh

And ye shall eat in plenty, and be satisfied, and praise
the name of the Lord your God, that
hath dealt wondrously with you: and my people
shall
never be ashamed.

27. aw attah yash yada ky ahayach al qarab al
yasharaAl aw ky ahayach Al Yachuwshauh
Naphash Alasham aw lah owd aw any am
yash lah buwsh

And ye shall know that I am in the midst of
Israel, and that I am the Lord
your God, and none else: and my people
shall never be ashamed,

28. aw yash hayach achar ky ahy shaphak any
ruwach al kol Basar aw Naphash ban aw
Naphash ban yash Naba Naphash zaqan
chanowsh yash chalam chalowm Naphash
bachuwr chanowsh yash raah chaazzayown

And it shall come to afterward, that I will pour out my
spirit upon all f lesh; and your sons and
your daughters shall prophesy, your old
men shall dream dreams, your
young men shall see visions:

29. aw gam al abad aw al shaphchah al
chammah yowm ahy shaphak any ruwach

And also upon the servants and upon the handmaids in
those days will I pour out my spirit.

30. aw ahy Nathan pala Al shamaym aw
al arats dam aw ash aw Tamarah ha ashan

And I will shew wonders in the heavens and
in the earth, blood, and fire, and pillars of smoke.

31. shamaym yash haphak al chashak aw
yaraach al dam panym gadal aw yara
yowm ha Yachuwshauh actar

The sun shall be turned into darkness, and
the moon into blood before the great and the terrible
day of the Lord come.

32. aw yash hayach ky Asar yash qara
     al sham ha Yachuwshauh yash Malat yth
     al har Tsyown aw al shalowm yash
     palatah hy Yachuwshauh yash amar aw
     al saryd Asar Al Yachuwshauh yash qara

And it shall come to pass, that whosoever shall call
on the name of the Lord shall be delivered: for
in mount zion and in Jerusalem shall be
deliverance, as the Lord hath said, and
in the remnant whom the Lord shall call.

CHAPTER 3

1. yth hannah al cham yowm av al ky ath
   ky ahy shuwb shabath ha yachadah
   aw shalam

   For behold, in those days, and in that time,
   when I shall bring again the captivity of Judah
   and jerusalem,

2. ahy gam acaph kowl Gowy aw ahy yarad s
   ham al amaq al yachashaphat aw ahy
   shaphat ayn cham sham yth any am aw yth
   any Nachylah yasharaAl Asar cham hayach
   puwts bayn Gowy aw chalaq any arats

   I will also gather all nations, and will bring
   them down into the valley of Jehoshaphat and will
   plead with them there for my people and for
   my heritage Israel, whom they have
   scattered among the nations, and parted my land.

3. aw cham hayach yadad garal yth any am
   aw ahayach Nathan yalad yth zanah aw Makar
   yaldah yth yayn ky cham Taqaph shathah

   And they have cast lots for my people;
   and have given a boy for a harlot, and sold
   a girl for wine, that they might drink.

4. aph aw Mah hayach attah halom asah owd ayn
   howy Tsara aw Tsydan aw kowl galylah ha
   Phalashath ahy attah shalam ayn gamal
   aw han attah gamal ayn qal Maharah
   ahy shuwb Naphash gamal al Naphash
   ratsan Rash

   Yea, and what have ye to do with me,
   O Tyre, and Zidon, and all the coasts of
   Palestine? will ye render me a recompense?
   and if ye recompense me, swiftly and speedily
   I will return your recompense upon your
   own head.

5. ky attah hayach laqach any kacaph aw
   any zahab aw hayach bow al Naphash
   haykal any Towb Machmad Mallah

   Because ye have taken my silver and
   my gold, and have carried into your
   temples my goodly pleasant things:

6. ban gam ha yachadah aw ban ha
   shalam hayach attah Makar halom yavany
   ky attah Taqaph rachaq al sham gadal

   The children also of Jadah and the children of
   Jerusalem have ye sold unto the Grecians,
   that ye might remove them far from their border.

7. hannah ahy uwr sham al ha Maqam sham
attah hayach Makar sham aw ahy shuwb
Naphash gamal al Naphash ratsan Rash

Behold, I will raise them out of the place whither
ye have sold them, and will return
your recompense upon your own head:

8. aw ahy Makar Naphash ban aw Naphash
ban al
yad ha ban ha yachaday aw sham yash
Makar cham ha shabay halom am rachaq
yth Yachuwshauh hayach dabar

And I will sell your sons and your daughters
into
the hand of the children of Judah, and they shall
sell them to the Sabeans, to a people far off:
for the lord hath spoken it.

9. qara attah hannah bayn Gowy qadash
Malchamah uwr Gabbor chanowsh yanach
kowl chanowsh ha Malchamah Mashak Nagash
yanach cham alah

Proclaim ye this among the Gentiles; prepare
war, wake up the mighty men, let
all the men of war draw near;
let them come up:

10. kathath Naphash ath al charab aw Naphash
Mazmarah al romach yanach
challash amar ahayach Gabbor

Beat your plowshares into swords, and your
pruninghooks into spears: let
the weak say, I am strong.

11. uwsh Naphash aw bow kowl attah Gowy
aw acaph Naphash yachad cabab sham
ky zah Gabbor ban halom yarad howy
Yachuwshauh

Assemble yourselves, and come all ye heathen,
and gather yourselves together round about: thither
cause thy mighty ones to come down, O
Yachuwshauh.

12. yanach Gowy uwr aw alah halom
amaq ha Yachuwshaphat yth sham ahy
yashab halom shaphat kowl Gowy cabab

Let the heathen be wakened and come up to
the valley of Jehoshaphat: for there will I
sit to judge all the heathen round about.

13. shalach attah al Maggal yth qatsar hy bashal
bow yarad yth gath hy Mala shaman
shuwq yth sham ra hy rab

Put ye in the sickle, for the harvest is ripe:
come, get you down: for the press is full, the fats
overflow; for their wickedness is great.

14. chaman chaman al amaq ha charats
yth yowm ha al Yachuwshauh hy Nagash
al amaq ha charats

Multitudes, multitudes in the valley of decision:
for the day of the Lord is near
in the valley of decision.

15. shamash aw yaraach yash qadar aw
kowkab yash acaph sham Nagahh

The sun and the moon shall be darkened and
he stars shall withdraw their shining.

16. Al Yachuwshauh gam yash shaag al ha
    Tsyown aw Nathan qowl day shalam
    aw shamaym aw arats yash raash
    han Al Yachuwshauh ahy Machacah ha
    Naphash am aw Maowz ha ban ha
    yasharaAl

The Lord also shall roar out of
Zion, and utter his voice from Jerusalem;
and the heavens and the earth shall shake:
but the Lord will be the hope of
his people, and the strength of the children
of Israel.

17. gam yash attah yada ky ahayach Al Yachuwshauh
    Naphash Alasham shakan al Tsyown any qadash
    har ky yash shalam chava qadash aw
    sham yash lah zuwr abar al Naphash kol
    owd

So shall ye know that I am the Lord
your God dwelling in Zion, my holy
mountain: then shall Jerusalem be holy, and
there shall no strangers pass through her any
more.

18. aw yash hayach al ky yowm ky al
    har yash Nataph yarad Tyrosh acac aw
    al Gabah yash yalak ayn chalab aw kowl
    aphyq ha yachaday yash yalak ayn
    shaqah aw Mayanah yash yatsa ha Bath
    ha Yachuwshauh aw yash shaqah amaq
    ha shattam

And it shall come to pass in that day, that the
mountains shall drop down new wine, and
the hills shall f low with milk, and all
the rivers of Judah shall f low with
waters and a fountain shall come forth of the house
of the Lord and shall water the valley
of Shittim.

19. Matsraym hayach shamamah aw Adam
    yash shamam Madbar yth chamac
    al ban ha yachadah ky cham hayach
    shaphak Naqa dam al sham arats

Egypt shall be a desolation, and Adam
shall be a desolate wilderness for the violence
against the children of Judah, because they have
shed innocent blood in their land.

20. han yachadah yash yashab alam aw shalam
    al Dar halom Dar

But Judah shall dwell for ever, and Jerusalem
from generation to generation.

21. yth ahy Naqah sham dam ky anky hayach lah
    Naqah yth Yachuwshauh shakan al Tsyown

For I will cleanse their blood that I have not
cleaned: for the Lord dwelleth in Zion.

CHAPTER 1

1. hayach come to
2. zaqan old
3. adam men
4. Nathan give
5. azan ear
6. yashab inhabitants
7. hayach hath
8. Naphash your
9. yowm days
10. caphar tell
11. yanach let
12. achar another
13. Dar generation
14. gazam palmerworm
15. yathar left
16. arbah locust
17. akal eaten
18. yalaq cankerworm
19. chacyl caterpiller
20. quwts awake
21. shakkor drunkards

22. bakah weep
23. yalal howl
24. shathah drinkers
25. yayn wine
26. yabash dried up, withered
27. Tyrosh new sweet wine
28. acac wine
29. charath cut off
30. pah mouth
31. alah come up
32. atsum strong
33. ayn without, with
34. Macpar number
35. Asar whose
36. shan teeth
37. aryach lion
38. Mathallaah cheek
39. labaowth great lion
40. shuwm laid
41. gaphan vine
42. shammah waste
43. qatsaphah barked
44. Taanah fig tree
45. aylan tree
46. asah made
47. Tahowr clean
48. chasaph maka bare
49. shalak cast away
50. sarag branches
51. labanah white

52. alah lament
53. bathuwlah virgin
54. chagar girded
55. saq sackcloth
56. baal husband
57. Nauwr youth
58. akal meat
59. Manchah offering
60. Nacak drink offering
61. sharath minister
62. abal mourneth
63. saday field
64. shadad wasted
65. dagan corn
66. yatshar oil, anointed
67. amal languisheth
68. buwsh ashamed
69. akkar husbandmen
70. yalal howl
71. karam vinedressers
72. chattah wheat
73. saowrah barley
74. qatsar harvest
75. abad perished
76. ramaman pomegranate
77. Tamar palm tree
78. ats trees, wood
79. ky because
80. shashon joy
81. cuwr away

82. adam men
83. Mazbaach altar
84. bow come
85. luwn lie
86. layal night
87. Mana withhold
88. qadash most holy, sanctify
89. Tsown fast
90. qara call
91. atsarah solemn assembly
92. acaph gather
93. zaqan elders
94. zaaq cry
95. ahabah love, alas
96. qarab at hand, with
97. shad Destruction
98. shadday almighty
99. Nagad before
100. anachnw ourselves
101. gyl gladness
102. paradah seed
103. abash be rotten
104. Tachath under
105. Magraphah clods
106. atsar garners
107. Mammagurah barn
108. harac broken down
109. Mah how
110. how
111. bahamah beast

112. anach groan
113. adar herds, flocks
114. baqar cattle
115. buwsh perplexed
116. Marah pasture
117. tsaown sheep
118. Madbar wilderness
119. lahabah flame
120. lahat burned
121. aphyq river
122. maym waters

CHAPTER 2

123. Taqa blow
124. shaphar trumpet
125. Tsyown zion
126. ruwa sound an alam
127. qadash holy, sanctify
128. har mountain
129. ragaz tremble, quake
130. bow cometh
131. qarah nigh
132. chashak darkness
133. aphalah gloominess
134. anoky I, me
135. anan clouds
136. Ab thick
137. shachar morning
138. paras spread
139. al upon
140. rab great
141. am people
142. atsum strong
143. sham there, thence, thither

144. alam ever
145. low neither
146. kol any
147. yacaph any, more
148. achar after, behind
149. shanah years
150. rabah many
151. Dar generation
152. panym before, face
153. sham them, name
154. ganan garden
155. adan eden
156. gam yea
157. palaytah escape
158. palatah escape
159. Marah appearance
160. parash horse man
161. ruwts run
162. qowl noise
163. Markabah chariot
164. rash tops
165. raqad leap
166. qash stubble
167. shuwm set
168. Malchamah battle, war
169. arak array
170. saggy much
171. chuwl pained
172. qabats gather
173. paruwr blackness

174. Gabbor mighty
175. alah climb up
176. chowmah wall
177. chanowsh men
178. yalak march, walk
179. chash every one
180. darak ways
181. abat break
182. arach rank
183. chash one
184. dachaq thrust
185. azrachy another
186. Gabar everyone
187. Macallah path
188. shalach sword
189. batsa wounded
190. bow enter
191. baad at
192. challown window
193. gannab thief
194. shamaym heavens
195. shamash sun
196. yaraach moon
197. qadar be black
198. kowkab stars, aprince
199. acaph withdraw
200. Nagahh shining
201. Nathan utter,
202. Nagad
203. qowl voice

204. chayl army
205. Machanah camp
206. Maod very
207. yara terrible, fear
208. Mah who
209. yakol can
210. kuwl abid
211. attah now
212. Naam saith
213. am even
214. bakah weep
215. Macpad mourning
216. qara rend
217. bagad garment
218. chanan gracious
219. racham merciful
220. arak slow
221. aph anger
222. charad kindness
223. Nacham repenteth
224. ra evil
225. shaar leave
226. barakah blessing
227. akal meat
228. qahal congregation
229. qabats assemble
230. zaqan elders
231. acaph gather
232. yanaq suck
233. shad breasts

234. yanach let
235. chathan bridegroom
236. yatsa go forth
237. chadar chamber
238. kallah bride
239. chappah closet
240. bayn between
241. kahan priests
242. Mazbaah altar
243. chuwc spare
244. alam porch
245. Nachalah heritage
246. charaph reproach
247. Gowy heathen
248. Mashal rule
249. amar say
250. bayn among
251. ayach where
252. Mah wherefore
253. qana jealous
254. chamal pity
255. zah thy
256. ahy I will, be
257. anah answer
258. shalach send, sent
259. shabaa satisfied
260. ath therewith
261. low no, not
262. uwd more
263. Nathan make

264. rachaq remove far
265. al off, into, toward
266. Rash head, from, forfront
267. Tsaphowny northen
268. chayl army, strength
269. Nadach drive
270. Tsyah barren
271. qadmowny east
272. cowph hinder part
273. achar utmost
274. baosh stink, a stench
275. alah come up
276. Tsachanah ill savour
277. gadal great
278. Mallah things
279. asah executeth
280. guwl be glad
281. shamach rejoice
282. dasha spring
283. Nasa beareth
284. pary fruit
285. Nathan yield, cause
286. Mowrah early rain, former rain
287. Tsadaqah moderately
288. yarad come down, bring down
289. gasham rain
290. Malqowsh latter rain
291. rashon first
292. chadash month
293. garan floors

294. Mala full
295. bar wheat
296. shaman fats
297. shuwq overflow
298. Tyrosh wine
299. yatshar oil
300. shalam restore render
301. shabaa be satisfied
302. halal praise
303. sham name
304. asah dealt
305. pala wonderously
306. ayn with
307. lah never
308. buwsh be ashamed
309. qarab midst
310. owd else
311. hayach come to pass
312. achar afterward
313. shaphak pour out
314. kol all
315. Naphash your
316. ban daughters
317. zaqan old
318. chalam dream
319. chalowm dream
320. chanowsh men
321. bachuwr young
322. raah see
323. chazzayown vision

324. shaphchah handmaids
325. Tamarah pillars
326. ashan smoke
327. haphak turned
328. al into
329. actar come
330. ashar ,Asar, whosoever, whom
331. qara call
332. al on the
333. Malat delivered
334. palatah deliverance
335. saryd remnant

CHAPTER 3

336. ath time, sign
337. shuwb, bring again, return
338. shabath captivity
339. amaq valley
340. shaphat plead
341. Nachylah heritage
342. Asar whom
343. puwts scattered
344. chalaq parted
345. yadad cast
346. garal lots
347. yalad boy
348. zanah harlot
349. Makar sold, sell
350. yaldah girl, damsel
351. Taqaph might
352. shathah drink
353. Tsara Tyre
354. Tsydan Zidon
355. galylah coast
356. phalashath palestine

357. gamal recompense
358. ratsan own
359. Rash head
360. laqach taken
361. kacaph silver
362. zahab gold
363. bow carried
364. al into
365. haykal temples
366. Towb goodly
367. Machmad pleasant
368. Mallah thing
369. yavany Grecian
370. rachaq remove far, far off
371. gabal border
372. uwr raise, wake up, be wakened
373. Maqam place
374. Asar whither
375. sham whither
376. shabay sabean
377. dabar spoken
378. qara proclaim
379. bayn among
380. qadash prepare
381. Gabbor mighty
382. yanach let
383. Mashak draw
384. Nagash near
385. alah come up
386. kathath beat

RICHARD JOHNSON

387. ath plowshare
388. qal swiftly
389. Maharah speedily
390. Mazmrzh pruninghook
391. romach spears
392. challash weak
393. Gabbor strong
394. uwsh Assemble
395. bow come
396. yachad together
397. cabab round about
398. yashab sit
399. shaphat Judge
400. shalach put
401. Maggal sickle
402. qatsar harvest
403. bashal ripe
404. yarad get down
405. gath press
406. Mala full
407. ra wickedness
408. rab Great
409. chaman Multitudes
410. charats decision
411. Nagash near
412. shaag roar
413. Nathan utter
414. qowl voice
415. raash shake
416. Machacah hope

417. Maowz strength
418. shakan dwelling
419. zuwr strangers
420. abar pass, son
421. al through
422. kol any
423. owd more
424. Nataph drop
425. yarad down
426. Tyrosh new
427. acac wine
428. Gabah hills
429. yalak flow
430. chalab milk
431. aphyq rivers
432. shaqah waters
433. Mayanah fountain
434. yatsa come forth
435. shamamah desolation
436. chamac violence
437. al against
438. shaphak shed
439. Naqa innocent
440. yashab dwell
441. alam forever
442. Naqah cleanse

www.ingramcontent.com/pod-product-compliance
Lightning Source LLC
Chambersburg PA
CBHW031300120626
46545CB00007B/2915

*9 7 8 1 9 5 8 4 3 4 6 4 2 *